... returned on or before

21879

HELP THE AGED

JULIA SHIPSTON
(SERIES EDITOR: ROB ALCRAFT)

First published in Great Britain by Heinemann Library
Halley Court, Jordan Hill, Oxford OX2 8EJ
a division of Reed Educational and Professional Publishing Ltd

OXFORD FLORENCE PRAGUE MADRID ATHENS
MELBOURNE AUCKLAND KUALA LUMPUR SINGAPORE TOKYO
IBADAN NAIROBI KAMPALA JOHANNESBURG GABORONE
PORTSMOUTH NH CHICAGO MEXICO CITY SAO PAULO

A 3% royalty on all copies of this book sold by Heinemann Library will be donated to Help the Aged, a registered charity, number 272786.

Produced by Plum Creative (01590 612970)
Printed in China

01 00 99 98 97
10 9 8 7 6 5 4 3 2 1

ISBN 0 431 02754 4

British Library Cataloguing in Publication Data
    Shipston, Julia
    Help the Aged. - (Taking Action)
    1. Help the Aged - Juvenile literature
    I.Title
    361.7'632

Acknowledgements
The publishers would like to thank the following for permission to reproduce photographs:
Helen Bayliss-Jackson pp10,11; Nick Hayes p28; Marcella Hugard pp12,13,18,19,22; Ute Koecher/HAI p24; Cheryl Martin p13; Midlands Electricity plc p15; Joe Partridge pp5,9,21,26,27; Mike Pattison p29,30; Douglas Quiggan p19; Rene Verharge/HAI p25; Andrew Webb/HAI p8; Yorkshire Post Newspapers Ltd p7; *and* Help the Aged p6,10,12,13,14,15,(16,17),20,23,29; HelpAge International pp8,24,25.

Cover photograph by Joe Partridge.
Cover illustration by Scott Rhodes.

Every effort has been made to contact copyright holders of any material reproduced in this book. Any omissions will be rectified in subsequent printings if notice is given to the publisher.

All words in the text appearing in bold like **this** are explained in the Glossary.

CONTENTS

WHAT'S THE PROBLEM?

All around the world, there are more old people than ever before. Better diets and medical treatment are helping people to live longer. By the year 2030 there will be nearly one and a half billion old people in the world, and a third of all the people who live in the UK will be over 60.

It is hard to imagine being old: perhaps not being able to walk easily; being scared to go out; or feeling lonely because you have no family around. It might be cold where you live, because there is not enough money to pay the electricity bill. You might be hungry, because there is not enough food.

Here are some of the things that older people have said:

'I live in a tower block and the lifts often break down. Then I can't go to the day centre because there is no way to get my wheelchair down the stairs. I get fed up when that happens.'

'Last week the light bulb went on the landing but I couldn't reach to put a new one in. I was scared in the dark.'

'Sometimes I go for a whole week without talking to anyone.'

'I can't go shopping because there's no shop or post office in my village and the bus only comes once a week.'

Help the Aged raises money to help with these problems and **campaigns** for changes to give all older people a better future.

This graph shows how the number of people aged 60 and over in the world is increasing.

Help the Aged is a charity which helps older people who are poor, frail or isolated.

Many thousands of older people are happy and healthy and able to do the things they want to do. Help the Aged works to make life better for all older people.

There are nearly 600 million people aged 60 and over in the world.

WHAT DOES HELP THE AGED DO?

Help the Aged was set up in 1961. One of its first tasks was to help older **refugees** who had lost their homes and families in a major earthquake in Yugoslavia.

Now it works in the UK and in 50 other countries around the world, through its international partner, HelpAge International.

Every year, Help the Aged raises around £50 million. This comes from gifts and **profits** from its shops. The **charity** also asks people to collect money from their neighbours and sends out letters asking for money. It also organizes events like bungee jumping where people pay to take part or they find **sponsors**.

▼ **Four-year-old Jimmy Sheals from London designed a Help the Aged collection envelope. He said his great-grandma was happy, but others were not so lucky.**

6

There are more than 10 million pensioners in the UK.

Children from Whingate Primary School in Leeds carry another load of cans to a recycling bin. Pupils at the school filled 10 sacks with cans for the Help the Aged Cash for Cans appeal within the first month of joining up! When these are sold, the money goes towards Help the Aged's work for frail and isolated older people.

One and a half million UK pensioners survive on social security benefits.

HOW DOES HELP THE AGED USE ITS FUNDS?

Help the Aged helps older people in lots of different ways. It builds special housing, where older people can be cared for and where they can live safely. It runs a free telephone helpline, so that older people can phone up and get advice about their problems; it sends out information on things like money, health and safety.

HELP AT HOME

Transport, such as special minibuses, is provided for people who can't get to the shops or to the doctor or even

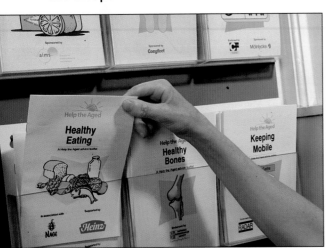

▲ **Help the Aged produces 23 different free advice leaflets about money, health and safety. Every year, more than two million older people ask for leaflets to be sent to them.**

visit friends. Telephone alarms are fitted in people's homes so that they can call for help if they fall down or feel ill, and door locks and smoke alarms are installed to make them more safe and secure.

Help the Aged also gives money to local groups working for older people. It helps them to set up clubs or provide services and buy big things like minibuses or small things like televisions for their clubs.

Older people sometimes feel that no one is very interested in their problems. Help the Aged goes out around the country and listens to them. Sometimes it works with other organizations to find the answers to problems.

SPEAKING OUT

Help the Aged speaks to the government about what older people have said they need. It also talks to newspapers and radio and television programmes about the things that affect older people's lives.

Half of all fatal accidents in the home happen to over 75-year-olds.

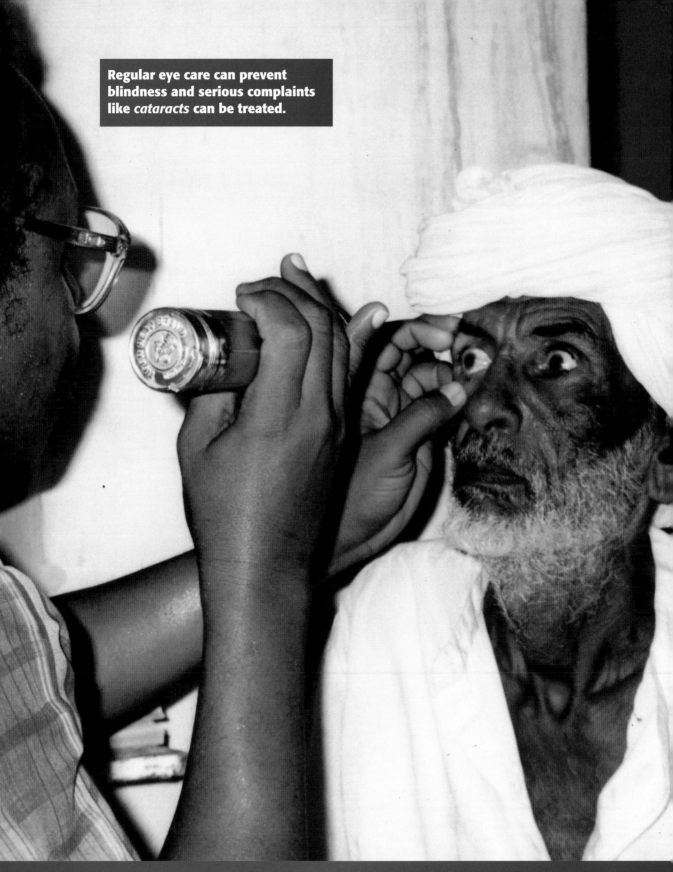

Regular eye care can prevent blindness and serious complaints like *cataracts* can be treated.

Help the Aged provides eye care to more than 10,000 older people in Asia and Africa.

MEET HELEN BAYLISS-JACKSON

SCHOOLS ORGANIZER

My job is to visit schools in the whole of south, west and mid-Wales.

I talk to young people of all ages – from infants up to sixth formers – about what it is like to be old, and what they can do to help older people.

There are more than a thousand schools in my area and I usually visit up to 20 a week. It's really hectic but I love it!

7.00am I'm due to talk to an assembly at a comprehensive school 80 km away, so after a quick breakfast I'm on my way.

9.00am I tell pupils about a paper boy who noticed that yesterday's paper was still in the letterbox where an old man lived on his own. He alerted neighbours who found that the man had fallen down.

I encourage young people to watch out for older people and to spend time with elderly friends and relatives. But it is important not to talk to strangers — only people you know.

▶ **If Help the Aged has ever visited your school, you will probably remember Hector the dog, the schools' mascot. He comes everywhere with me.**

1½ million older people are lonely at the weekend.

11.00am It's time for a tutorial with some sixth formers, where we discuss in detail some of the problems faced by older people. Then it's time to go to an infant school to tell them a story. Before they go back to their classes they all want to give Hector a cuddle!

It's St. David's Day – an important anniversary in Wales. Many school children dress in Welsh national costume to mark the day. I'm here to collect money that the children raised for Help the Aged, so I've put my special outfit on too!

1.30pm I'm at a local junior school now, where we are working on a play about a couple who fall in love, get married and have children. The children later have families of their own and move away, leaving the old couple alone. We talk about the things that frighten old people like the possibility of burglars, being ill or having an accident. We try to imagine how they feel and what they might need. This play usually makes everyone laugh when they see their friends in wedding outfits or cuddling babies!

3.00pm Next it's 'work-out' time at another junior school where pupils have been sponsored to take part in 'Hectorcise', an exercise and dance routine.

There is just time to call at a school which has collected money for Help the Aged and have a photograph taken by the local paper, so everyone can see how hard the pupils have worked to collect such a lot of money. Then it's time to go home and do all the paperwork.

Hector is wearing a special jumper today, with cats on it. He wants to show that not all dogs are the same and some actually like cats! Not all old people are the same, either. Everyone likes to be treated as an individual.

11

MEET BARBARA KENNEDY

SENIOR CARE WORKER

I help to look after the residents at one of Help the Aged's homes for older people at Moor House in Middlesex.

There are 25 people living here. They are aged from 67 to 95 and although some are quite **frail** they are all very lively! It is always busy, with friends and family coming and going and lots of activities taking place during the day.

All the care assistants work different hours to make sure some of us are here all through the day and night. That means I sometimes have to sleep here. But today I am starting work straight after breakfast.

▶ **Some of the residents need a bit of help with washing and dressing.**

8am The first thing I do is talk to the care workers who have been here during the night, to catch up with everything that has been happening. Everyone has had breakfast in their rooms. I go round and help anyone who needs a hand with washing, having a bath, or getting dressed.

10.20am Time for tea! Afterwards there will be lots of things going on – like armchair exercises or arranging a session with the hairdresser who comes in once a week.

12.30pm We have lunch together in the dining room. All the residents have their own rooms but we like to get together during the day.

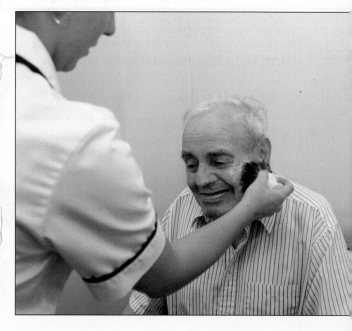

Help the Aged spends £2 million a year on special minibuses.

Sometimes people just want to have a chat. They may want to discuss a problem or share a joke. Having a friend to talk to can make a big difference to older people's lives.

The afternoons are fun — we might play bingo, take part in a quiz, or do craft-work or painting. Some of the residents like to play cards or take part in a sing-song. Others might like to go for a walk or look round the gardens. Sometimes we go out in the minibus on a trip to the countryside or to do some shopping.

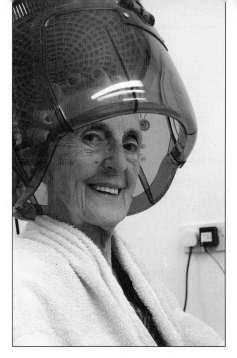

The hairdresser's visits are always very popular. It cheers people up to know they look nice.

3.30pm During the afternoon we take the tea trolley round again — we must get through gallons of tea each day! It's good to have a sit down. The residents might want to have a chat or ask our advice about **pensions** or any problems they may have.

5.30pm We have tea and sandwiches together in one of our lounges and in the evening we watch television, talk, or read.

9pm It is time to make sure everyone is back safely and to talk to the night staff who will be taking over now. It has been busy day, but it is rewarding work. I like to think I have been a friend to all the older people who live here.

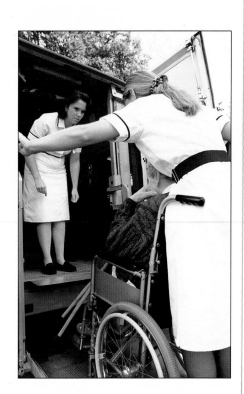

Our minibus has been specially adapted to take wheelchairs so we can all go out together on trips and no one has to be left behind.

13

Nearly ½ million older people in the UK live in residential or nursing homes.

MEET HELEN EDWARDS

VOLUNTEERS MANAGER

You may have been in one of Help the Aged's **charity** shops at one time or another. They sell clothes, books and toys which have been given to us. I can't pass one of our shops in case I miss a bargain!

Our shops rely on 4000 **volunteers** who are not paid for their work, but do it to help the charity. It's my job to make sure we have enough volunteers and that they like working for us. Otherwise they might not come again!

Another part of my job is to find ways for Help the Aged to work with other charities so that we can help older people together. Today I am involved in both these things.

9.00am I go to a Help the Aged shop in Kentish Town in north London. We have to plan for Volunteer Recruitment Week. We hold this event every year to encourage more volunteers to come and work in our shops. We have posters and badges and hold parties in the shops.

The volunteers in the shops do lots of different jobs. First they have to sort through all the things that people have given to us. They have to be careful, though. Once they found a hedgehog — fast asleep and curled up in a plastic bag. They clean and iron clothes, mark prices, make displays in the window and work on the till. It's hard work, but our volunteers say they enjoy it very much. Some may be lonely at home, so it's a good way of meeting other people.

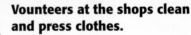 **Vounteers at the shops clean and press clothes.**

14

200,000 volunteers help collect money for Help the Aged.

12.00am – 5.00pm After talking to the volunteers, it's back to Help the Aged for a meeting with another charity, Action for Blind People. We are trying to raise money for elderly blind or partially sighted people to have a seaside holiday. We take them to special hotels with proper facilities.

Many of these people haven't had a holiday for a very long time. One lady, 75-year-old Clara Lingwood, told us: 'A holiday would be a relief from loneliness, as there would be the company of others. I can't get out on my own. I would appreciate it very much.' If I can help people like Clara, I reckon my job is pretty special.

▲ Through the Promenade Appeal, these blind and partially sighted people were able to have a holiday in special hotels where they felt safe and secure.

► Television presenter Philip Schofield visited one of our shops in Southampton to meet the volunteers who work there.

◄ Here I am at a huge balloon race in Birmingham, held as part of the Promenade Appeal.

9 out of 10 blind or partially sighted people are over the age of 60.

MEET HUGH ROONEY
HOME SAFETY FITTER

Help the Aged's HandyVans are special vans driven by trained fitters who install home safety and security equipment free of charge to older people. Help the Aged has already fitted this equipment in more than 10,000 homes.

I am one of Help the Aged's fitters and my job is to visit up to three homes a day, making them safe and secure. I drive a special van with all the tools, locks and alarms in the back.

I have travelled all over the world working as a carpenter and joiner, but the job I do now is the most satisfying. Many older people are very vulnerable, especially if they live on their own. A lot of the houses I visit are unsafe and have no locks on the windows or doors. This makes people worry about burglaries.

9.00am Today I visit Mr and Mrs Crewe, who live in Speke, Liverpool. They learned about the HandyVan scheme at one of Help the Aged's shops, and asked for me to call.

Together we go round the house and see what is needed to make it safe. We decide on new locks for the back door and windows and a smoke alarm. Sometimes I fit door chains and spy holes, too.

16

Nearly 2 million older people find it difficult to do simple jobs like hoovering.

11.00am Tea break! One of the good things about this job is that I'm always given a cup of tea. Often I'm offered biscuits, bars of chocolate and sweets too! People are very grateful to have the work done and want to say thank you.

Mr and Mrs Crewe don't need anything else to be done, but often I will do other jobs for people, like changing a light-bulb or repairing a dripping tap. Many older people are too **frail** to manage these small jobs. But having them done can make a big difference to their lives.

The work does not cost anything for the older people. But to see the relief on their faces when their jobs are done and their home is secure, is worth a million dollars to me.

1.00pm I've got two more calls to do this afternoon. I do a lot of travelling, as my area covers the whole of Merseyside, but I'll probably make it home by 5.30pm.

I am showing Mr and Mrs Crewe how the smoke alarm works. This will warn them if a fire starts in their home.

Fitting a lock to Mr and Mrs Crewe's back door. They said they would feel safer and sleep better now.

17

WORK IN THE COMMUNITY

Many older people find it difficult to leave their homes. It may be hard for them to walk or to get on and off buses. If they are stuck indoors all day with no one to talk to, they often become very lonely.

GETTING OUT

Help the Aged is involved in many projects to help older people get out and meet others. It helps local groups to buy special minibuses so that older people can travel to day centres or go on shopping trips or outings. One group used the money to buy a special bus with its own kitchen and tables and chairs. The bus picks people up from their homes and then they can all have lunch together inside it! The **charity** also gives money to help people start up things like village care clubs, where older people meet at the village hall for exercise or games, or to go on outings.

AT HOME

Many older people enjoy living in their own homes, and being

▲ **Help the Aged helps buy minibuses so that people can go shopping or on outings.**

independent. Help the Aged gives money to projects which help them with things like home repairs and gardening.

Another way Help the Aged makes people feel safe and secure in their homes is to provide SeniorLink telephone alarms. People can use these to call for help if they feel ill or frightened.

Half of the people aged 75 and over live alone.

▲ **Money from Help the Aged** helped set up this day club at West Preston Manor, where older people can take part in lots of activities – including keeping fit.

▶ **With these special telephone alarms** people feel safe and secure in their homes, knowing that help is just a telephone call away.

Help the Aged has fitted over 30,000 telephone alarms in older people's homes.

WORK IN INFORMATION

Actor Richard Wilson takes a break from *One Foot in the Grave* to record a radio appeal asking people to give money for *cataract* operations.

One of the main things that older people need is more information. They need to know what money they can claim from the government, or how to make their homes safer.

ADVICE

Help the Aged sends out advice leaflets and runs a free telephone information service called SeniorLine. This answers questions from older people and those who care for them. In the winter, it tells people how to keep warm.

PUBLICITY

Help the Aged wants everyone to understand what life is like for older people. People from the **charity** often appear on television and radio programmes to talk about what older people need.

Sometimes, there is a big problem, like how to help older people who live in remote villages and towns, where there are few doctors, buses or shops. Help the Aged invites people to meetings so they can share their good ideas.

More than a million older people do not claim all the benefits they are entitled to.

It can be difficult to get to the shops when you live outside the town. Help the Aged held a series of *conferences* to talk about the problems of growing old in the countryside and what can be done to make life easier for older people who live in remote areas.

Staff at Help the Aged's free telephone advice line, SeniorLine, can help advise older people about the extra money they can receive if they are in need.

£800 million a year of benefits are left unclaimed by pensioners.

WORK IN HOUSING

Sometimes older people can no longer manage to live on their own. They may be very **frail** or need some nursing care. Sometimes they are lonely and want to live with other older people. Help the Aged provides different sorts of places where they can live.

It runs nine **residential homes** where older people are cared for 24 hours a day. They can get help with things like dressing or having a bath. All their meals are cooked for them. Doctors, **chiropodists** and hairdressers visit, and there is a minibus to take people shopping and on trips.

 Sometimes older people are frail and need nursing care.

More than four million older people in the UK have some form of disability.

SHELTERED ACCOMMODATION

Some older people prefer to live in **sheltered** accommodation. These are small flats where people can be more **independent** and shop and cook for themselves. Some have staff who also live there, to help the residents if they need it. Other sheltered housing schemes are for more active people who keep an eye on each other.

▼ **The actors Dame Judi Dench and her husband Michael Williams, came with their daughter to the Chelsea Flower Show, to open Help the Aged's garden. This garden was designed for an active retirement. It has a studio for painting or drawing.**

GARDENS

Help the Aged knows that gardens are important to older people, too. Many older people like gardening and enjoy having somewhere pleasant to sit outside. Every year the **charity** shows a garden especially designed for older people at the Chelsea Flower Show. Sometimes it is a small garden for sheltered housing. One of the gardens shown at Chelsea was specially designed for a new home which Help the Aged is building at Luton.

23

A third of all older people have difficulty with their hearing.

WORK OVERSEAS

▼ Help the Aged set up the Eye Department at Zanzibar Hospital six years ago, but now local people run it themselves.

Help the Aged works in many countries around the world, helping when there are disasters and emergencies, providing healthcare and eye treatments and raising money for projects which help older people to help themselves. It also sets up organizations in these countries to work with their own older people.

The old ways of caring for grandparents within the family are breaking down. Many young people have left home in search of a better life. Tens of thousands of young adults have died of **AIDS**-related diseases, leaving older people on their own or caring for grandchildren.

Ronnie Graham works for Help the Aged in Tanzania in Africa. This is how he spends some of his week.

Monday I'm off to the hospital in Zanzibar to talk to the people who run the Eye Department there. Local people have been trained to run it – we always make sure the projects we start can be carried on by local people.

Tuesday I drive to an old people's home. Money from the **charity** has been used to rebuild it. A hundred people live there. Some have suffered from leprosy, like 90-year-old Maryam, who has no fingers or toes and is blind. Before we started work, everyone slept in one big room. There were no toilets. Now there are separate rooms and proper bathrooms.

Health projects across the world prevent illness as well as treat it.

Wednesday I get up early to catch the plane to Lake Victoria. It is 16,000 km away. From there I fly another 480 km to the **refugee** camp at Karagwe.

In 1994 around two million people left the next door country of Rwanda because of the fighting there. Today I am visiting two camps where 200,000 of these refugees live. We give clothes, medicine, water and cooking pots to all refugees over 50 years old. Our workers in the camps train **volunteers**, give out blankets, take people to the clinic and organize different activities.

It is a three-hour drive to the next camp. Because we are going through bandit country, armed policemen come with us.

Friday I'm back from the camps in the afternoon – and then it's time for dancing! All the team members go out together on Friday nights to see a band called Shikamoo. The charity helped the band to start and now it plays at events around the world to raise money.

The disabled and older people have a very hard timè in the refugee camps. It is difficult to keep walking or waiting in long queues.

When people 'Adopt a Granny', they give money each month to make sure these 'grandparents' have food, shelter and medical treatment. Sometimes the money pays for big projects, like a water pump for an old people's home in Zimbabwe, or repairing homes damaged by earthquakes in Colombia.

17,000 older people in developing countries have been 'adopted' by families in the UK and Europe.

RELYING ON COMMUNITY TRANSPORT

Many older people cannot use public transport. They may find it difficult to walk to the bus stop, or the steps onto the bus might be too high. Perhaps they are in a wheelchair.

If people are stuck indoors all day, with no one to talk to, they can feel cut off from everyone. Without transport, it is difficult to do everyday things such as shopping, collecting their **retirement pension** or visiting the doctor.

GETTING ABOUT

Help the Aged helps in lots of different ways. It might help one group to buy a special minibus which can take people in wheelchairs. Another group might need money to start a dial-a-bus scheme. This is when people can telephone to ask for a special bus to collect them from their home. The **charity** also helps projects where **volunteers** use their own cars to take people out.

▼ **Irene lives on her own in a bungalow in south London and cannot get out on her own because it is very painful for her to walk.**

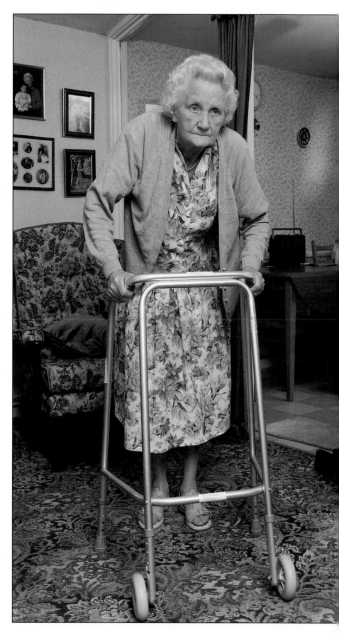

1 in 20 older people spend Christmas alone.

Irene, who will be 81 this year, would be a prisoner in her own home if it weren't for a special minibus which picks her up every day to take her to her local day centre. Sometimes the neighbours pop in to check that she is all right. But until she started going to the day centre, Irene was very lonely.

LOTS TO DO

There are lots of different things to do at the centre, like weaving, pottery or cookery. People can join in some singing, play bingo or darts, or take part in a quiz. Often Irene just wants to talk to her friends there. They choose what they want for lunch and sit down to eat a hot meal together. This, says Irene, is one of the most important things about coming to the day centre. 'I get a good meal here. If I was at home I probably wouldn't bother to cook for myself.'

A hairdresser visits the day centre, and there is a bathroom for people who need help to take a bath. A volunteer visits three times a week to see what shopping people would like. The day centre has two minibuses to collect people and take them home and another minibus which takes people shopping and on outings.

▲ A special bus comes to collect Irene, drop her off at the day centre and bring her home again.

▲ Irene enjoys a good meal and catches up with her friends at the centre. After they have finished their lunch they are going to play bingo.

27

Many older people get no presents on their birthday.

VISION FOR THE FUTURE

> Help the Aged is working with the Royal College and the Royal Society of Arts on the DesignAge Project to improve the design of everyday objects such as furniture, transport or packaging to make them easier to use.

It is hard to imagine what the world will be like when you are grown up. What kind of transport will there be? Will you still want to go out to see your friends or will you talk to them on a **videophone** instead? And what about shopping – will you be able to do it from your computer?

PLANNING AHEAD

These are the sort of things that Help the Aged has to think about. As well as helping older people now, it must plan ahead and think about what they will need in the future.

This might mean better designed houses, to make the lives of older people more comfortable and secure, or public transport which is easier for everyone to use. Improved services like Meals on Wheels or Home Helps would mean that older people get the help they need to live independent lives. Help the Aged also wants to ensure the future of **retirement pensions**, so that no one has to go without the basic necessities. Above all, it wants older people to feel needed and valued and to know that they are an important part of society.

A baby boy can expect to live until 74 years old and a baby girl until nearly 80.

SHARING A LIFETIME'S EXPERIENCE

Being old isn't just about problems. Older people have a wealth of talent and knowledge which come from a lifetime's experience. Sharing that experience with others brings benefits to both older people and future generations.

Many older people want to go back to work. Help the Aged is involved with the **charity** Third Age Challenge which helps them do this.

Help the Aged is taking part in the Millennium Awards Scheme, which gives money to people aged 60 and over who live in rural areas, to set up projects to share their skills. These projects will enable older people to help each other.

Some older people enjoy working in schools, helping young people with their lessons or making history come alive by describing events they lived through. Others pass on their talents in the workplace, helping younger staff cope with new jobs.

▼ **Many older people have worked hard all their lives, either in their jobs or bringing up a family. They want to continue to be useful. Help the Aged is involved with the charity Third Age Challenge which helps older people back to work.**

By the year 2000 nearly one in six of the population will be a pensioner.

FURTHER INFORMATION

Children at several schools in the UK worked on a Help The Aged project which involved talking to older people to find out what life was like 50 years ago. It helped them understand old people a lot better. This is what they said:

'I never used to be friendly towards old people – I didn't know, I thought they were like witches.'

'I feel better about old people now – I always thought they were not nice to talk to, but after talking to my uncle I think they are really interesting.'

Many schools organize fund-raising events or get involved in projects to help older people in their communities. Help the Aged's schools organizers can tell you about the things you can do, too. We hope you will welcome them into your school.

Schools can contact Help the Aged's office in Leeds for special information packs. Write to: Help the Aged, Unit 7, Kirkstall Industrial Park, Leeds LS4 2AZ.

If you have elderly friends or relatives, they can get advice from SeniorLine, Help the Aged's free telephone advice line for older people, their friends, carers and family. It is open from 10am to 4pm, Monday to Friday. All telephone calls are confidential and free. The SeniorLine number is 0800 650065.

Six pupils from Sneyd High School in Newcastle-under-Lyme formed a Community Support Group to help elderly and disabled people in their area. They were given a special Tunstall Caring Award at Help the Aged's Golden Awards party by television personality Lionel Blair.

GLOSSARY

AIDS Auto Immune Deficiency Syndrome. It means that the body is not able to fight illness or infection.

campaign work to draw attention to the things you believe in

cataract a kind of filmy skin that covers the eye and stops people from seeing. It can be removed in a simple operation.

charity a non-profit-making organization set up to help those in need

chiropodists people who care for your feet and keep them comfortable and healthy

conferences events where a lot of people can get together, have meetings and hear talks about a particular subject

fatal causing death

frail weak or in poor health

independent able to look after yourself

isolated feeling alone, with no-one to turn to for help or to talk to; or living somewhere that is far away from other people and facilities

pensioner a woman over 60 or a man over 65

profits money that is extra and doesn't have to be spent on running a business or paying people's salaries

refugee someone who has had to leave home because of war or natural disaster, or because of being bullied or threatened, and who moves to another town or country

residential home a place where people live, sleep and eat

sheltered housing grouped houses or flats for active older people, sometimes with a warden nearby

social security benefits financial help from the government for people without enough money

sponsor someone who promises to pay money for a person taking part in an activity or event

retirement pension a scheme of saving money – people set aside money while they are working, then use it when they have stopped working.

videophones telephones that let you see the person who is talking to you

volunteers people who work without being paid

INDEX